THE LITTLE BOOK OF
Restorative Justice
for
Older Adults

THE LITTLE BOOKS OF JUSTICE & PEACEBUILDING

Published titles include:

The Little Books of Justice & Peacebuilding present, in highly accessible
form, key concepts and practices from the fields of restorative justice,
conflict transformation, and peacebuilding. Written by leaders in these fields,
they are designed for practitioners, students, and anyone interested in justice,
peace, and conflict resolution.

The Little Books of Justice & Peacebuilding series is a cooperative effort
between the Center for Justice and Peacebuilding of Eastern Mennonite
University and publisher Good Books.

THE LITTLE BOOK OF
Restorative Justice
for
Older Adults

*Finding Solutions to the Challenges
of an Aging Population*

JULIE FRIESEN AND WENDY MEEK

Good Books
NEW YORK, NEW YORK

Good Books books may be purchased in bulk at special discounts for sales promotion, corporate gifts, fund-raising, or educational purposes. Special editions can also be created to specifications. For details, contact the Special Sales Department, Good Books, 307 West 36th Street, 11th Floor, New York, NY 10018 or info@skyhorsepublishing.com.

Good Books is an imprint of Skyhorse Publishing, Inc.®, a Delaware corporation.

Visit our website at www.goodbooks.com

10 9 8 7 6 5 4 3 2 1

Library of Congress Cataloging-in-Publication Data

Names: Friesen, Julie, author. | Meek, Wendy, author.
Title: The little book of restorative justice for older adults: finding solutions to the challenges of an aging population / Julie Friesen, Wendy Meek.
Description: New York: Good Books, 2017. | Series: Justice and peacebuilding
Identifiers: LCCN 2017022558 | ISBN 9781680992083 (paperback)
Subjects: LCSH: Older people--Legal status, laws, etc. | Old age assistance—Law and legislation. | Older people—Services for. | BISAC: LAW / Alternative Dispute Resolution.
Classification: LCC K646 .F75 2017 | DDC 344.03/2682—dc23
LC record available at https://lccn.loc.gov/2017022558

ISBN: 978-1-68099-208-3
e-ISBN: 978-1-68099-209-0

Printed in the United States of America

Table of Contents

SECTION I
Foundations of Restorative Justice with Older Adults

1.
Introduction

How will our family decide who will be power of attorney for our parents?

When will Dad move out of his home and into long-term care?

We can't have Mom living with us anymore because it's just too hard.

Why are my children fighting over where I will live?

Why is my son taking money from me?

These are challenging questions that many older adults, their families, and communities are increasingly asking as the population ages in North America and around the world. Population data has been discussed in catastrophic terms: untenable health-care costs, exhausting pension funds, and a crisis in at-home care and long-term housing. Certainly, there are significant strains on older adults, their families, and our communities. However, these pressures, given the right responses, also create opportunities for better relationships and healthier communities. We believe approaches based on restorative justice principles will abundantly support individuals, families, and communities through these challenges.

This *Little Book of Restorative Justice* examines the use of restorative justice to respond to situations of conflict and abuse involving older adults. Restorative justice offers older adults, their families, caregivers, and other people in their lives a safe, respectful *process* to assist in resolving conflict and abuse. Restorative justice practices, such as restorative dialogue, can help older adults and their families talk constructively and safely in order to move forward together.

Our Journey

We, the authors, work for Community Justice Initiatives of Waterloo Region (CJI) in Ontario, Canada. CJI is a nonprofit organization known worldwide for starting the first victim-offender mediation program. During CJI's history, the organization has continuously responded to community needs by creatively and innovatively applying restorative justice principles to new situations. One of CJI's programs, the Elder Mediation Service (EMS), is geared toward older adults who have experienced conflict, crime, or abuse.

At CJI, we got involved with restorative justice programming with older adults in early 2000, through Arlene Groh, a nurse and case manager at a Community Care Access Centre (CCAC) who specialized in situations of suspected elder abuse. Arlene's experiences led her to connect with CJI and other community partners to find an innovative way to work with our aging population. Arlene found that in many of the

4

elder abuse and conflict situations, criminal charges were not possible or appropriate. The reasons older adults did not report to the police were complex. Many situations stemmed from experiences of historically difficult and conflictual relationships. Even in relationships where they had been taken advantage of or where abuse had been involved, most of the older adults did not want to involve the justice system for fear of losing relationships. The older adult may have relied on the person causing harm for help. They likely loved the person (often a family member) and did not want them to "get into trouble." Additionally, some were afraid of reprisal.

Arlene's frustration with the limited options that she was providing older adults led her to seek a different way to address and prevent these situations. She was interested in restorative justice but could not find any projects that used it to respond specifically to conflict and abuse involving older adults. As a result, Arlene organized a collaborative process that included agencies who provided services to seniors, interested community members, ethno-cultural community leaders, older adults, and Community Justice Initiatives to create a restorative justice process that responded to elder abuse. Arlene's vision led to the Restorative Justice Approaches to Elder Abuse and Mistreatment Project. The project piloted restorative justice as a way of addressing elder abuse. The restorative justice services were provided by Community Justice Initiatives. The project experienced successes, challenges, and many opportunities, with the final report acknowledging that the community was now better able to respond to elder abuse situations.[1]

When the pilot project ended in 2004, CJI continued to operate a restorative justice service for older adults under its Community Mediation Services (CMS) program umbrella. As the demand for elder-specific services continued to increase, CJI received funding to create the Elder Mediation Service (EMS), a new specialized program that uses restorative justice approaches to respond specifically to situations of elder abuse and conflict. In CJI's Elder Mediation Service, program staff and volunteers speak daily with older adults and their support networks about abuse and other highly complex conflict situations. We have had continuous exposure to people at the end of their lives who are isolated and heartbroken at the loss of family relationships, and we understand the importance of reconnecting people to repair relationships and diminish social isolation. As a result of our work, we also know the relief and joy that can blossom when abuse has been addressed appropriately and conflict has been resolved. Relationships can be transformed! Through our work in Elder Mediation Service, we are able to help families reconnect with each other and build a stronger, more inclusive community.

Relationships can be transformed!

Community Justice Initiatives' understanding of restorative justice work with older adults owes much to the vision and passion of Arlene Groh. She subsequently wrote a book on the initial project's learnings entitled *A Healing Approach to Elder Abuse and Mistreatment: The Restorative Justice Approaches to*

Elder Abuse Project (2003). She continues to travel the world, talking about her work and modeling restorative justice approaches in her training. Her book is a must-read for individuals interested in approaching older adult conflict, crime, and abuse situations from a restorative perspective. You can connect with her at www.healingapproaches.com.

What This Book Will Discuss

The following describes the central ideas explored in each chapter. We hope you will join us on a journey to discover the opportunities of restorative justice processes with older adults.

Section I: Foundations of Restorative Justice with Older Adults

In **Chapter 2,** we will describe restorative justice, identifying goals and "signposts." We will tell you about different tools that we use to help people be at their best in difficult situations (restorative circles, mediation, social groups, etc.). We will also discuss limitations: circumstances where we should be cautious about using restorative justice practices with older adults.

In **Chapter 3,** we discuss the importance of involving community and challenging ageism in our restorative justice work.

In **Chapter 4,** we explain issues specific to working with older adults. Like any other application of restorative justice in a particular area (e.g., with schools or with survivors of sexual abuse), we need to understand the unique needs of older adults so that, together, we can create processes that fit our participants and communities.

After the first four foundational chapters, we continue the dialogue of restorative justice and older adults with case studies and specific examples.

Section II: Case Studies of Restorative Justice with Older Adults

In **Chapter 5**, we will examine a case study of elder abuse. We will define elder abuse and talk about how we use restorative justice in situations of abuse. We will describe the situation of elder abuse and explain how the older adult, family, and community created a restorative justice process. We will discuss the outcomes and talk about further learnings when approaching elder abuse from a restorative justice perspective.

In **Chapter 6**, we will describe situations where adult siblings struggled with decision-making regarding the lives of their parents. We will describe how a restorative process needs to ensure that the older adults' autonomy is paramount. We will discuss how a restorative justice process worked and what the outcomes were in this situation.

In **Chapter 7,** we will discuss a situation of caregiver burnout, how this situation was addressed by a restorative justice process, and the outcomes. We will discuss how the restorative justice process is used when approaching caregiver conflict.

In **Chapter 8,** we will describe a community in conflict: a housing complex with a significant amount of conflict among residents. Here we illustrate our "whole housing complex" strategies where we use our tools to help residents resolve micro-conflict and work with all residents to create a sense of community within the building. This is a new way that we are involving community in restorative justice processes.

In **Chapter 9,** we will reflect on the common themes demonstrated by our case studies. These themes will point us toward an age-friendly community where a restorative response is the first response. We will invite you to think about how to make this vision a reality.

Why Use RJ with Older Adults?

We have found that restorative justice practices have many positive outcomes. Using a restorative justice process empowers older adults, creating a safe space for them to talk about conflict and abuse in their lives while respecting their autonomy and decision-making abilities. The process provides opportunity for accountability and finding meaningful, concrete ways to work toward "making things right."

The restorative justice process also allows for an understanding that conflict and abuse happen in relationships and that the impacts ripple through family, friends, and community networks. We involve many people in the restorative justice processes, including family members and friends of the older adult. These processes acknowledge that family and friendship connections are important, even if they are abusive or damaged by serious conflict. The processes create opportunities to repair harm and move forward in a healthy way.

> **Restorative justice empowers older adults.**

9

In evaluating our restorative justice service, we have noted very positive and practical outcomes for older adults. These outcomes include:

- older adults live in safe and conflict-free environments,
- healthier relationships are created with caregivers and neighbors,
- the older adult's community becomes more aware of the older adult's and caregiver's needs,
- the older adult accesses meaningful services that help them connect to their immediate communities,
- and participants enhance their communication and self-advocacy skills.

How to Use This Book

This book is for people who are new to restorative justice and looking to understand basic principles, as well as for restorative justice programs that are interested in designing a service specifically for the needs of older adults. We also wrote this book for older adults and their families who are looking for ways to have their needs addressed.

We hope you will be inspired to use restorative justice to respond to the challenges of an increasing population of older adults in your own community. We hope you use the individual case studies to consider how you could help older adults to meaningfully address the complex situations that create stress and unhappiness in their lives. We also hope that you not only work with the individual situations of conflict and abuse, but look to create a community where

10

older adults' rights are preserved and their autonomy is respected. We believe that the use of restorative justice along with other community services will reduce the isolation of older adults by helping people reconnect and reconcile after conflict, crime, or abuse. We have seen restorative justice work to build lasting relationships that are able to withstand difficult life circumstances and benefit the entire community.

2.
Restorative Justice

In this chapter, we will briefly touch on the criminal justice system in addressing elder abuse, describe a restorative justice approach, explain the restorative justice tools we use with older adults, describe the characteristics of a restorative justice practitioner, and conclude with a discussion of situations in which we should be cautious in using a restorative justice approach.

The Criminal Justice System and Elder Abuse

Near the end of their lives, older adults are sometimes physically or mentally vulnerable and dependent on others for care. In some situations, older adults may fear for their safety, their well-being, and their finances. Sometimes the police are called to respond to circumstances of elder abuse. Where a person who has perpetrated abuse is found guilty, a punishment is determined by the criminal court system. Consequently, in some cases, the justice system is able to protect older adults from further abuse. In fact, there are times at Community Justice Initiatives

(CJI) when we will consult with and refer to our local Elder Abuse Response Team (EART), which is made up of police and social workers who determine if a criminal charge should be laid as a way to support the older adult, their family, and caregivers.

However, in our experience, older adults usually hide experiences of abuse, and when they are revealed, they do not want to call the police. Why? The most common answer is that the older adult does not want to lose the relationship with the person who is abusing them—often because they rely on that person for help, or they care for that person and want to protect them.

Arlene Groh, whom we discussed in Chapter 1, recollects a financial-abuse situation where the mother refused to contact the police, even though she knew her son was stealing her money. Arlene was the family's caseworker and had given the mother contact information for the police. The mother did not want police involvement because her son "was a good man and probably needed the money more than her." She also needed him to help with her care, to buy groceries, and to take her to church each Sunday. The relationship with her son and his family was more important to her than the $40,000.00.[2] Certainly, there are also different situations where an older adult may not contact police because they are afraid of reprisal from the person causing harm.

There are other reasons why the justice system may not be the best system to address conflict and abuse experienced by older adults. Even though there are criminal code offenses to combat the abuse of older adults, there are barriers within North American justice systems that create difficulties when prosecuting situations of crime against older adults. Ageism is a significant barrier for older adults and often means that they are viewed as an unreliable witness due to being "forgetful" or "incompetent." Also, it can be difficult to get the necessary evidence to convict the person who has harmed the older adult because the older adult may not want to testify or may be unable to testify due to health reasons.

Restorative justice processes offer a different way of responding to conflict and harm, often allowing an older adult to address a situation that allows for growth and the positive transformation of relationships.

Restorative Justice: What is it?

Restorative Justice is a philosophy or worldview. The roots of restorative justice are found in the religious and spiritual traditions of many peoples around the world, particularly Indigenous peoples.[3] What we will discuss in this book is Community Justice Initiatives' vision of restorative justice philosophy.

There are many definitions of restorative justice. **A simple definition is that restorative justice is a non-adversarial, non-retributive approach to justice that emphasizes healing in victims, meaningful accountability of offenders, and the involvement of stakeholders—victims, offenders, and communities—in creating healthier, safer communities.** However, the real power of restorative justice goes beyond this definition. The power of restorative justice is in the process people undertake as they seek to restore what they feel has been lost, whatever that may be. During the process, as people move together toward restoration, they often

14

experience self- and relational transformation. An effective restorative process encourages transformation in how people view harms and needs, their own roles and responsibilities, and their connections to each other.

Another way to understand restorative justice is by identifying the goals or "signposts" of restorative processes. In *The Little Book of Restorative Justice* (2014), Howard Zehr suggests that the goals of restorative justice practices are to: involve everyone, to the fullest extent possible, who has a stake in the situation and outcome; identify and address the harm that has occurred; identify the obligations that people have to each other and provide the opportunity for those obligations to be addressed; identify and address the needs that have arisen; and involve the community in meaningful ways.[4] Zehr translates the goals into "signposts" because they are nonprescriptive, pointing participants in a general direction without necessarily telling them how to get there.

> An effective restorative process encourages transformation in how people view harms and needs, their own roles and responsibilities, and their connections to each other.

Zehr's restorative justice signposts:

1. *Focus on the harms of wrongdoing rather than the rules that have been broken.*
2. *Show equal concern and commitment to those victimized and those who have offended, involving both in the process of justice.*
3. *Work toward the restoration of those harmed, empowering them and responding to their needs as they see them.*
4. *Support those who have offended, while encouraging them to understand, accept, and carry out their obligations.*
5. *Recognize that while obligations may be difficult for those who have offended, those obligations should not be intended as harms, and they must be achievable.*
6. *Provide opportunities for dialogue, direct or indirect, between those harmed and those who have harmed, as desired by both parties.*
7. *Find meaningful ways to involve the community and to respond to the community bases of crime.*
8. *Encourage collaboration and reintegration of both those who are harmed and those who harmed, rather than relying upon coercion and isolation.*
9. *Give attention to the unintended consequences of actions and programs.*
10. *Show respect to all parties—those harmed, those who harmed, their friends and loved ones, and justice colleagues.*[5]

Our case studies in Chapters 5, 6, 7, and 8 will provide some real-life examples of processes that follow restorative justice signposts. However, there are many ways to implement restorative justice. A number of models have developed, unique to the specific cultural context of the community within which the model is operating. It is important for communities to have ownership over their own restorative processes. Thus, as Zehr writes, "Restorative justice should be built from the bottom up, by communities, through dialogue, assessing their needs and resources, and applying the principles to their own situations."[6]

At CJI, we have found the above goals and signposts to be invaluable when deciding whether to use a restorative justice process for a situation of conflict or harm. If a process cannot move in the direction of the goals or signposts, it is a strong indicator that perhaps restorative justice is not suitable.

Putting Philosophy into Practice

In our restorative justice work, we use a three-step process and a number of tools to assist older adults, their families, caregivers, and others to address conflict, crime, and abuse.

A) Steps of Restorative Justice

Step 1: Assess Readiness—We first meet individually with all people involved to assess readiness, determine if they are interested in participating, and prepare them for the next steps. In this preparation meeting, we ask participants questions such as:

- Does the older adult need any support around disabilities or health concerns?
- Do any of the participants require support from other agencies, family members, faith communities, or friends (i.e., who else needs to be involved)?

17

- Do the participants have any safety concerns about participating before, during, or after the process?
- Is the older adult able to communicate their needs, process the information, and participate in negotiating an outcome (and do they need support around this)?
- Are people willing to take responsibility for harms that have occurred?
- What happened and what has been the impact on those who are involved in this situation?
- What do participants need that would help them move forward and feel safe?
- What has been tried before to resolve this situation?
- What can the participants offer for the development of a plan for moving forward?
- Is there some object of value (i.e., a photograph, a memento, etc.) that participants would like to bring to the circle?

Step 2: Bring People Together—In most situations, or where safe and appropriate, after we meet individually with all participants, we bring people together for dialogue to help resolve conflicts or heal harms. Generally, all of our restorative justice tools have a process that participants work through together.

Introduction:
- Participants introduce themselves and talk about the object of value they brought (see above) and why it is meaningful to them.
- Participants set guidelines and values that will guide the process.

- Participants give a short story of how they are connected with the older adult.

Dialogue:
- Participants dialogue together about what happened.
- Participants identify their needs and discuss how these needs can be addressed.
- Participants identify options or ideas about outcomes.
- Participants discuss what they could contribute to resolving the issue(s) and how they can work toward "making things right" between them.

Agreement:
- An agreement (memorandum of understanding) is written, and all participants consent to following it. Agreements can include outcomes such as: a restitution plan, apologies, setting up a new power of attorney, living arrangements, monitoring relationships with the older adult, safety plans, follow-up meetings, etc.

Step 3: Follow Up—After bringing people together, we have follow-up meetings with participants. It is important to periodically evaluate the usefulness of a service, as well as determining if other assistance is required. Following up allows us to measure whether our process is reflective of restorative justice goals and signposts.

- Were participants empowered to identify their own needs?
- Were needs met?

- Were participants encouraged to accept responsibility for their actions?
- Were people accountable directly to each other?

The job of the facilitator is to seek to inspire and support a safe environment where people can communicate fairly, frankly, and openly about needs and responsibilities. Reaching agreement is not as important as supporting a safe process. Often, simply by meeting together, people see each other differently—understanding and respect emerges, as does the capacity to work through differences. The participants are restored to a place where they can again be caregivers, friends, and/or family without feeling that relationships have been fractured beyond repair. Everything may not be resolved and everyone may not be at peace, but a restoration of some sort usually occurs.

The job of the facilitator is to support a safe environment and process.

B) Tools of Restorative Justice

The following is a brief description of the different restorative tools we use to help people work through conflict, crime, and abuse.

Mediation: Mediation is a voluntary process that encourages individuals in conflict to sit down together to understand each other's perspectives. At CJI, mediations are facilitated by a roster of trained volunteer mediators from our community who are supervised by our staff. *Mediation is best used* when participants have specific needs that can be addressed through a negotiated agreement. It is also a good strategy when there are only two or three individuals impacted by a conflict situation. *Mediation is not the best* process when there has been abuse or when there is a significant power imbalance.

Peacemaking Circles: A Peacemaking Circle is a process that gathers together a group of people as equals to have difficult yet respectful dialogues. A "talking piece," an object of importance to the participants, is used to give everyone an opportunity to speak and be heard.

- The talking piece is passed, in turn, from person to person around the circle.
- Only the person holding the talking piece is allowed to speak, although a participant might choose to pass or remain silent when it is their turn.

A peacemaking circle also usually uses "ceremonies," such as a poem or a prayer, at the beginning and end of the circle to inspire feelings of connectedness. Peacemaking Circles are geared towards larger and more deep-seated issues that involve a larger number of participants (e.g., conflict between distinct groups in a housing complex). The circle creates a safe space to discuss difficult issues in order to improve relationships and resolve differences. It actively works to engage individuals to work on building a deeper understanding of the community

21

before getting to the issues that are contentious. There are many different types of circles, including talking circles and healing circles. *Peacemaking Circles are best used* when there are many people impacted by a situation. The peacemaking circle can also be used where there has been abuse and significant power imbalances. *Peacemaking Circles are not the best* when time is limited or when a quick solution is required. For a deeper discussion of peacemaking circles, refer to Kay Pranis's *The Little Book of Circle Processes* (2005).[7]

Conflict Coaching: Conflict Coaching teaches conflict resolution, communication, and problem-solving skills to people who are struggling to effectively resolve conflict. Conflict coaching encourages individuals to examine their own conflict styles and patterns and how their own behavior can de-escalate conflict and promote harmony, even if the other participant has not changed their conduct. *Conflict coaching is best used* before or during mediation or peacemaking circles in order to better equip individuals with the skills they need to work successfully in conflict resolution processes. Conflict Coaching is also used by individuals seeking to manage their own personal conflictual situations but who may not be able or interested in participating in a mediation or peacemaking circle.

Other restorative justice processes deal less with direct conflict and harm and more with community-building and prevention. CJI uses some of the following tools when working in older adult residential settings in order to equip people with the skills and abilities to be at their best.

Education Groups: Education Groups are organized around specific topics to help people learn about and share ideas. Generally, these groups run for 6–8 weeks and are facilitated at older adult residences, recreation centers, faith settings, and other places where older adults gather. Education groups are usually on specialized topics, including communication, recognizing and managing conflict, appreciating diversity, and so on. Often, other community services (such as multicultural centers and counseling agencies) join the education groups to communicate their expertise and connect their services to older adults.

Social Groups: Social Groups help people better connect to each other in a social setting by encouraging friendships while enjoying a common recreational or artistic activity (such as gardening groups, game nights, etc.). These groups are initially facilitated by CJI, then run on their own with tenants leading the activities.

Mediation and Peacemaking Circle Workshops: Mediation and Peacemaking Circle Workshops train older adult residents to resolve conflicts themselves. Part of the purpose is to create a team of older adult mediators and peacemaking-circle keepers who can help resolve future conflicts.

Support Groups: Support Groups are gatherings created for older adults who are going through similar situations and are looking for support. Support groups are formed around a specific issue that a number of people are experiencing (for example, loss of a relative). They are often organized and sometimes facilitated by CJI, but the content is often created and managed by the residents.

Restorative Justice Practitioners

Just as important as knowing the goals, signposts, and tools of restorative justice is having an effective practitioner or facilitator. *Restorative justice requires practitioners who are creative and flexible*, able to respond meaningfully to unique situations and challenges.

Practitioners need to invite creativity, openness to new ideas, and flexibility so that we create processes that work for participants' unique needs. A good practitioner also knows that, while it is their responsibility to keep a process true to goals and signposts, restorative justice is ultimately about participant needs and decision-making. Practitioner ego must be contained.

A skilled restorative justice practitioner would rather listen than speak yet can intervene when needed to create the space for participants to engage in dialogue that allows them to communicate their needs and hear and respond to the needs of others.

Responding to anger: There are situations where participants become very angry during a dialogue. Restorative justice practitioners remain calm and need to act quickly to defuse the potential for violence. The practitioners must respond to all participants' feelings of safety while continuing to respond to the needs of an angry participant. One facilitator stays with the group to communicate what is happening and determine how they are feeling. The other facilitator meets with the angry participant, away from the rest of the group, if it is safe. People feel anger for many reasons, but one common cause in restorative justice practice is that the process is not meeting their needs. The restorative justice practitioner first helps them calm down by giving them space to vent in a safe way. If they are able to calm down, the restorative justice practitioner asks what is working for them about the process and what is not. Often, changes to the process can be made, such as shuttling back and forth between participants. Changes can help defuse anger and re-engage participants positively in the process.

When multiple people describe a single incident, there will be multiple, often contradictory, stories or "truths" told. *A good restorative justice practitioner is open to many different truths* and can accept that these truths often exist together in contradiction. They maintain a nonjudgmental attitude, but also acknowledge that they may be prey to certain biases, including connecting with one person more than others. The facilitators will recognize and reflect on these feelings privately (or with colleagues) and seek to manage them so that they do not impact the process.

The restorative justice practitioner views every situation from a learning perspective, meaning that they know they do not have all the answers. An effective practitioner presents as calm, empathetic, and engaged in the process. The restorative practitioner also connects with everyone in a kind way—in that they demonstrate care for everyone and look for the good in everyone—even though one may have an unpleasant personality or may have seriously hurt someone. We have discovered that these practitioner characteristics are essential to quality restorative process.

A good listener:
- Has a relaxed and open body posture
- Is warm and inviting
- Refrains from suggesting solutions
- Asks open-ended questions
- Summarizes and reflects back to participants
- Validates emotions and perspectives without agreeing with them
- Refrains from over-identifying with their own life
- Allows for silence
- Comes from a perspective of being curious instead of judgmental
- Looks for nonverbal cues
- Checks in regularly to see if people are OK

When should we be careful about using restorative justice processes?

We have learned from our years of practice that restorative justice is *not* appropriate for every situation. The following are situations where we either would not use a restorative process or would proceed with caution and modify our approach.

1. The person who has harmed another is not prepared to be accountable.

We are cautious about proceeding with restorative justice processes when the person who has harmed refuses to be accountable for their actions. We have been involved with some very complex situations, including situations of elder abuse when the person who has harmed an older adult does not acknowledge their responsibility. We usually refer these situations to our local Elder Abuse Response Team (EART), which includes police and social workers. This team will meet with families to determine if a criminal charge is appropriate. Sometimes, we will still stay involved but will not bring the person who has harmed the older adult into the process as this can create new psychological harm and the potential for further abuse for the older adult. Instead, we bring together the other caregivers, friends, professionals, and the older adult to talk together in a restorative process so that everyone hears the same information about what has occurred. This is a situation where we use peacemaking circles to give caregivers and the older adult the opportunity to share their feelings about the information they have heard and come to a joint understanding about next steps. Usually, the restorative process results in plans for safety and empowers others who care for the older adult to recognize what is happening so that they can assist with the plan that has been put in place for the older adult's safety.

2. People cannot advocate for themselves and do not have advocate supports.

When someone is not in a place where they can express what they need to repair harm or move forward with what feels good to them, restorative justice is not appropriate. This could be in situations where an older adult has mental health or cognitive difficulties. However, in some cases, there are ways to assist people to express or articulate needs, including bringing an advocate who knows them well, whom they trust. If someone does not have an advocate, then we help find one. We often connect people with professional and other informal supports, including self-help groups and spiritual groups, depending upon their comfort with these services. After these supports are in place, we can bring their advocates into the restorative process. The advocates can have different roles; for example, an agency who offers services to older adults, or a doctor, can bring information relevant to the older adult's health condition, thus educating the family to prepare them to discuss the future care of the older adult. Another example would be to include a caseworker from a home healthcare service who could share with the family about the older adult's care schedule.

In situations where someone has a health issue that limits capacity for participation, such as dementia, they can either designate an advocate or we can help them find one before we move ahead with a restorative process. In these situations, we *always* still involve the older adult with dementia. Providing service to the older adult with dementia is essential because we are acknowledging the capacity that they have to contribute to the restorative process and we are assisting the other participants in the restorative process to focus on the best interests of the older adult. In these situations, we talk with caregivers, professionals, and the older adult to ensure that we have done the work to involve the older adult in a way that is comfortable for them and that helps them be at their best. We further discuss health and dementia-related issues in Chapter 4.

3. There are violent trauma and power imbalances.

Engaging in a restorative process where one of the parties has experienced domestic violence or sexual trauma is both a controversial and delicate topic in the field of restorative justice. Although there is tremendous debate among practitioners on the appropriateness of restorative justice in cases of sexual trauma or domestic violence, it stands firm that in such cases significant consideration and care should be put in place if a process is to proceed. Restorative justice dialogue is not always an appropriate response. Ensuring that the safety, support, agency, and voice of the victim is protected throughout is foundational to any response.

One of the concerns of using restorative justice in the aftermath of domestic violence or sexual trauma is the power differential between participants. In abusive situations, power is used in a negative way—to control, to intimidate, to create fear—by the person who uses violence over the person victimized. Those who advocate for the use of restorative justice as a response to violence understand that, where safe and appropriate, where adequate assessment of readiness has taken place, restorative justice dialogue allows people who have been victimized an opportunity to feel empowered, to stand up to the person who has caused harm, and to share how their life has been affected.

Zehr's empowerment signpost is the guideline. The goal is to combat or minimize power imbalances. Another restorative justice researcher, John Braithwaite, suggests that the goal is to achieve empowerment to the extent that an environment of "non-domination" is achieved.[8] A strong restorative justice process carefully considers and monitors the degree to which participants feel safe and respected and ensures the process is proceeding in a way that parties agree is safe and reflects their needs. For more on restorative justice as a response to sexual abuse, see *The Little Book of Restorative Justice for Sexual Abuse* (2015)[9].

Even where abuse has not occurred, the presence of power or coercion between conflicting parties needs to be considered. Power in conflict situations can be understood as one party's ability to act, to influence, or to demonstrate resistance in the process.[10]

In older adult restorative justice processes, although it is recognized that there can be varying degrees of power between members of the parties (due to physical, mental, or economic capacities, family history, power of attorney responsibilities, etc.), it is important to ensure that everyone holds an adequate amount of power so that they can effectively participate.[11] In other words, it is not so much about who holds power, but an awareness of power and how it is used in the process and relationship.

Safeguards should be implemented to address power imbalances. Practices such as regular individual meetings, coaching, or including support people all help create a more equal power arrangement.

Restorative justice dialogue should be used in response to abuse only with voluntary participation of all parties, where a person who caused harm takes responsibility, where facilitators have adequate understandings of the impacts of abuse, and where adequate preparation, support, and safety planning has occurred. In the aftermath of many abuse situations or where power differentials are too great, restorative justice dialogue will not be appropriate.

4. The participants are wanting to be involved in criminal or civil court proceedings and restorative justice processes simultaneously.

It becomes very difficult to help families who are struggling with conflict, crime, and abuse involving an older adult when they are also involved in criminal or civil court processes. If restorative justice processes are used at the same time as retributive processes, we find that people are drawn to act in ways that do not help the restorative process. People may become tempted to use the restorative justice process as a way to gain information to use against another in the court process—a tactic that works well in court but undermines the truth-telling that is crucial in restorative processes. Also, the goodwill that is gained between restorative justice participants is often lost when the same people meet each other in court because the court process requires people to outline deficits in each other's character and behaviour. We do not use the participation in civil and criminal court as a hard rule to refrain from beginning restorative justice processes, but experience tells us that it is difficult for people to be involved in activities from both approaches at the same time. We usually suggest that people continue with the court processes and when they are completed, if they are still interested in restorative justice, that they contact our service, or, conversely, that people suspend the court process while restorative justice work is tried.

Next Steps

Now that we understand the important principles of restorative justice, the tools we use to implement principles, and the situations wherein we need to be cautious in using restorative justice, we are ready to think about how to create strong communities and address the systemic effects of ageism.

3.
The "Big Picture"
Creating Healthy Communities and Challenging Ageism

In the previous chapter, we described the philosophy, tools, and practices of—as well as barriers to—restorative justice. While restorative justice has been a positive intervention on a small scale, with older adults, their families, and caregivers, we struggle to impact some of the larger social forces—such as the isolation of older adults and attitudes of ageism—that create the need for our services in the first place. Our hope is that restorative justice continually allows us to think bigger, even as we focus on the individuals involved in our services. That is, as you read this book, we invite you to think about two main concepts: first, the importance of a strong and caring community, and second, the importance of challenging ageism. We reflect again on these ideas in Chapter 9 as we look to the future.

Community Is the Key to Success

Strong community connections create strong people. The quality of connection an older adult can make to their immediate community makes a huge difference in their well-being. Ultimately, restoring or creating community connections is a fundamental goal of restorative justice programs. When more of the people who care about an older adult know that conflict and abuse is occurring, there is a larger network of people committed to practically supporting an older adult and their caregivers. A significant aspect of restorative justice is that it connects and strengthens caring networks of support.

Strong community connections create strong people.

Connecting with Community

Community can mean different things to different people and does not just refer to the immediate family and friends of an older adult. A broader concept of community includes those who live in close proximity (neighbors) and also those who we do not call friends but with whom we feel a sense of connection due to shared beliefs, attitudes, or interests (such as people involved in our faith groups, social clubs, or sports teams). We also see an even larger definition of community as those who live in our city or town—those who we meet but do not know well. At Community Justice Initiatives (CJI), we have found that one of the most important and most difficult parts of our work is to help our participants create strong connections to this broader definition of community.

At CJI, we have observed the positive impact of community building, especially in our work at retirement homes and supportive housing

Creating community connections is a fundamental goal of restorative justice.

units for older adults. At the request of landlords, we started mediating conflicts between neighbors. What we soon discovered was that we had to return frequently to the same residence to respond to persistent conflicts between multiple neighbors. It occurred to us that, in order to effect lasting change, we would have to help the residents connect in a healthy way with their neighbors. They needed to believe in their own power or capacity to build a strong and healthy community. This realization influenced the types of tools we used in our practice, relying less on mediation and more on community-building events (for example, barbecues, social groups, and restorative circle processes) to build shared community values. After some time, we noticed that we were being called less frequently to address conflicts between neighbors. So what changed? While there were still noise complaints and arguments about dog droppings, communities were strengthened—there was an increased amount of understanding, cohesion, and empathy and the possibility for healthier and stronger social networks, plus the capacity to resolve their own issues.

Another way that restorative justice involves the community is to involve them directly in facilitating processes. CJI equips and supports well-trained volunteers to co-facilitate our restorative justice programs. Even though the service is not "for them," we hear from our community volunteers that their lives have changed as a result of helping others work through difficult situations.

"Working as a volunteer at Community Justice Initiatives has been quite life-changing for me. Every time I have the privilege to sit with people who are working through difficult situations, it never ceases to amaze me what I learn about myself. People come to the table sometimes in the most trying circumstances and are willing to show their vulnerability and transparency to come to a meaningful outcome, so that healing can begin for all parties. Every time I bear witness to these conversations, I walk away a better human being. I am becoming more conscious of how I interact with people both in my personal life and professional life. Allowing people a chance to be heard and understood is the beginning of transformation both in their lives and the lives of their family and friends. This ripple effect is what I believe will change our world."[12]
—a volunteer with Community Justice Initiatives

Finally, at the request of older adults, lawyers, nurses, religious representatives, home-care providers, seniors' advocates, and other important members of an older adult's community have all contributed at various times to the outcome of an intervention.

Restorative justice has an inherent ability to change a community. By participating in a process for another individual, community members are often impacted and transformed.

Challenging Ageism by Valuing Older Adults' Dignity and Autonomy

One of the more difficult aspects of our work is to seek to influence the larger social systems and cultural understandings that surround aging where we work in North America. The persistent negative stereotypes of older adults serve to undermine the autonomy and even safety of many older adults. Building community connections counteracts ageism.

We know that North America has a growing population of older adults. According to Statistics Canada, in 2011, one in seven Canadians is aged 65 or over, and by 2036, almost one in four Canadians will be an older adult.[13] In the United States, in 2013, older adults comprised 14.1% of the population, and by 2021, this number is expected to grow to 21.7% of the population.[14] With an aging population, many predict a drain on resources and a strain on communities. Predictions that use terms such as "drain" and "strain" indicate the perspective that older adults are a burden on society. If this is our outlook, it is easy to

Building community connections counteracts ageism.

arrive at a place where older adults' contributions to society are not valued or respected. As community builders, we take a different standpoint on the aging of the population, and we are not alone.

Some groups who share our perspective are working to create municipalities that intentionally work to help older adults age successfully with autonomy, respect, support for physical and mental challenges of aging, and an expectation that older adults are important, contributing members of communities. For example, where we live in Waterloo Region, Canada, several of our regional municipalities are working toward becoming an "Age-Friendly City (AFC)." According to the World Health Organization, "In an age-friendly city, policies, services, settings and structures support and enable people to age actively by: recognizing the wide range of capacities and resources among older people; anticipating and responding flexibly to ageing-related needs and preferences; respecting their decisions and lifestyle choices; protecting those who are most vulnerable; and promoting their inclusion in and contribution to all areas of community life."[15] Arlene Groh, the elder abuse and restorative justice consultant who helped found our service, is working to make the City of Waterloo, Ontario, Canada, an AFC as one strategy for preventing elder abuse. Arlene explains, "The impetus for Waterloo's AFC initiative is the recognition that elder abuse is a social justice issue, which requires intervention at the micro, meso, and macro levels. As a practitioner, I witnessed firsthand the impact on older adults of inadequate social policies affecting older people that can result in conditions that increase the risk of elder abuse. However, Age-Friendly Cities promote policies, services, settings and structures to support and enable all people to age safely."[16] Initiatives like Age-Friendly Cities and Restorative Communities (which we will discuss in Chapter 9) help communities prepare for the challenges of an aging population. We would have less older adult conflict, crime, and abuse if we lived in an age-friendly environment.

Ageism is the "stereotyping of and discrimination against individuals or groups based on their age. Ageism can take many forms, including prejudicial attitudes, discriminatory practices, or institutional policies and practices that perpetuate stereotypical beliefs."[17] Ageism also intersects at times with other isms such as racism and sexism, creating multiple layers of systemic discrimination for some older adults. Tackling ageism is challenging. In our restorative justice programming with older adults, we believe it is important to confront ageism with two strategies:

1. developing processes that build upon respect, dignity, and autonomy, and
2. challenging caregivers, professionals, and community members' often subconscious ageist assumptions.

Our work always stresses the importance of understanding and "keeping true" to the values of dignity and autonomy. At CJI, we talk about these values through a lens of **respect**: "not *to* you or *for* you, but *with* you." Our restorative justice process is firmly rooted in honoring everyone's **dignity**, their personal values and preferences, and their **autonomy**, or ability to determine and control their own affairs

Respect = not *to* you or *for* you, but *with* you!

and choices. Adhering to values ranges from the voluntary nature of our restorative justice services to our respect of someone in spite of "bad" choices. People respond by being open and truthful because they know the restorative justice processes are not judging their guilt or innocence.

Inherent in the values of dignity and autonomy is our care for the rights of older adults to have decision-making power over their lives, to participate actively in implementing actions that directly affect their well-being, to have their housing facilities respect their beliefs, to live free of abuse, and to be valued for their contributions to our community.[18]

In our work, it is important to be especially mindful of protecting the rights of vulnerable persons. We know that society often discriminates against older adults. Our service seeks to create equity, ensuring inclusion of the older adult and their advocates in decision-making. One of the concrete ways we do this in peacemaking circles is by providing the older adult with the opportunity to speak first *and* last.

We use our position as facilitators to help families, professionals, and other caregivers consider the dignity and autonomy of older adults. Often, we are cautioned by families or professionals to not involve the older adult in the restorative justice process. They are acting from a caring perspective, but they assume the participant will not be able to contribute to the discussion or that they will become overwhelmed. Another example from our experience is that, as people age, they are often infantilized; older adults are "cared for" similarly to a child that does not know "what is best for them." In fact, some adult children who seek out our services have not even considered informing their aging parent of their decision to contact us.

Our work attempts to replace isolation and ageism with connection and belonging by using strategies to enhance the power of older adults and to highlight the rights of seniors. Through respect, dignity, and autonomy, we hope that we are creating communities that value older adults.

4.

The Impacts of Aging

Preparing Restorative Justice Practitioners to Work with Older Adults

In this chapter, we describe the impacts of aging and identify practical strategies to consider when providing restorative justice services to older adults.

At Community Justice Initiatives (CJI), we train volunteers to be able to facilitate restorative justice processes like mediation and peacemaking circles. It is important that facilitators understand issues related to aging and their impact on how we implement restorative justice. Although issues of aging are often talked about in relation to illness and loss, we prefer to think about aging similarly to Maggie Kuhn, founder of the Gray Panthers, who declared, "Age is not a disease. It is strength and survivorship, triumph over all kinds of vicissitudes and disappointments, trials and illnesses."[19]

Understanding Aging: Biological, Social, and Psychological 101

The World Health Organization's (WHO) *World Report on Ageing and Health* describes aging in biological terms: "the gradual accumulation of a wide variety of molecular and cellular damage."[20] The report continues, "By age 60, the major burdens of disability and death arise from age-related losses in hearing, seeing and moving, and non-communicable diseases, including heart disease, stroke, chronic respiratory disorders, cancer and dementia."[21] These concerns may also be exacerbated by many factors, including several chronic conditions experienced at the same time and the lack of access to medication and other medical aids (hearing aids, etc.).

While considering the decline of our physical bodies is commonly discussed in conjunction with aging, it is just as important to emphasize the psychological and sociological impacts of aging. Older adults often experience psychological feelings of loss, whether due to loved ones' illnesses or deaths, the loss of their independence and decision-making, changes in residence, or other factors. This can lead to depression, low self-esteem, and anxiety. These psychological impacts can increase the likelihood that older adults become socially withdrawn, isolated, and at risk of suicide. The sociology of aging tells us that there are socially approved ways to age, that familial and community relationships will change as many older adults disengage, and that attitudes and beliefs (e.g., ageism) affect the well-being of older adults. The chart below identifies some concrete examples of the impacts of aging. Of course, none of these are the same for everyone, nor do they change at a predictable pace or at a specific age, as gender, ethnoculture, socioeconomic status, and other variables impact such changes.

Biological Impacts of Aging	Psychological Impacts of Aging	Sociological Impacts of Aging
Deterioration of muscle and bone density leading to reduced physical capacities.[22]	Increased feelings of loss due to death of relatives and friends.	Many older adults may be forced to retire once they reach the age of 65.
Loss of hearing and vision. [23]	Natural body changes increase a person's chances of experiencing chronic depression.[24]	Older adults begin to disengage from society and interact socially on fewer occasions.
Even with a heathy brain, significant brain volume will be lost through the aging process.[25]	Negative emotions, such as loneliness and anxiety, can lead many older adults to socially withdraw.[26]	Ageism occurs in many aspects of the older adult's life: age barriers in the workplace, withdrawal from medical interventions due to age, etc.[27]
Negative, age-related changes to the immune system, otherwise known as immunosenescence.[28]	Older adults are at a higher risk of suicidal thoughts.[29]	Older adults who are not as capable of using technology are unable to access vital information.[30]

When discussing the impacts of aging, we should not only do so in negative terms of loss, but also in the positive gains of experience and knowledge.[31] A restorative justice approach honors older adults as people with wisdom gained through life experiences. On one hand, a facilitator will need to consider the impacts of aging as it affects a person's capacity to participate in restorative justice. On the other hand, a facilitator will need to find ways to validate the contributions that older adults are uniquely capable of making.

> **A restorative justice approach honors older adults as people with wisdom gained through life experiences.**

How Can We Provide Service That Values Older Adults?

There are several practical strategies to help service providers acknowledge the specific issues of aging, while working in ways that value respect, dignity, autonomy, and ultimately, resolution and healing.

1. Do not take things personally.

People who are experiencing stressful situations of conflict, crime, and abuse may present as irritable or unwelcoming and may engage in difficult verbal behavior. This may be especially so with older adults who are experiencing feelings of loss and depression. The psychological impacts of aging can lead to a variety of expressive behaviors, including irritability, anger, and withdrawal. While we work to ensure that everyone (both volunteers and participants) feels safe, we also teach volunteer facilitators that negative behaviors are not often directed at them; it is likely the older adult's method of communicating unhappiness with their current situation or a way of reacting to feelings of powerlessness. Of course, if participants become verbally abusive, there are limits to how we'll allow ourselves or our volunteers to be treated.

2. Practice patience and excellent communication skills.

Often, as service providers, we want to be efficient with our time and our program participants' time. However, in our experience working with conflict, we have come to value the use of silence and patience. Sometimes, we have acknowledged that our service's most valuable contribution to the resolution of a conflict has been to provide the space for people to take their time to communicate with each other. This becomes even more valuable when communicating with older adults who may be experiencing hearing and vision loss, or may already be the recipients of impatient and dismissive behavior due to stigmas rooted in others' ageist beliefs. Practically speaking, it is important to speak slowly, clearly, to not eat while speaking, and to face the person you are speaking to when communicating. It is also important to be a patient and excellent listener. In general, an effective restorative justice practitioner should listen more than speak.

3. Be aware of older adult's body language and check out what you observe.

When communicating with older adults, be mindful of tiredness and be respectful of indications that the older adult wants the session to end. Tiredness can impede an older adult's capacity to advocate for themselves and make good decisions. Generally speaking, shorter meetings are best. When noting a shift in body language, make sure to ask the older adult if your observations are right. Check in with them often to ensure that they remain present, empowered, and prioritized in the process.

4. Be aware of issues of memory loss and keep it simple.

Memory loss is a common barrier for many people as they age. Memory issues often become exacerbated under stress, which is a common symptom of high-conflict situations. Under stress, many people have difficulty thinking clearly and remembering with ease. As a practitioner, it is important to be mindful of stress and memory loss and to use short sentences with easy words to ensure understanding. For all participants, and especially for older adults struggling with memory loss, try to simplify concepts and instructions, speaking clearly but not in a patronizing manner. For all participants, it is important to stick to one topic at a time and regularly ask if you should explain things again or in different ways. Help participants write things down so that they have something as a reference or a way of remembering. Also, always encourage participants to contact you if they have questions.

5. Avoid distractions.

It is good practice to limit auditory or visual distractions such as loud rooms, ringing phones, or high traffic spaces where people are coming and going, so all participants can concentrate more easily. Too many distractions make it difficult to hear and concentrate on the situation at hand.

6. *Be aware of your own body language.*
People who are involved in conflict, or in the aftermath of crime and abuse, need someone to talk to about what is happening or has happened. It is important to not rush through an older adult's story and to be an attentive listener. With your body, slightly lean in toward the older adult, and give frequent indications that you are following along with what they are saying, without taking over the conversation. It is also important not to overreact to difficult information that has been shared. Instead, stay calm and allow the older adult to have a sense of safety in continuing to share their information.

7. *Respect different ideas than your own and avoid ageist assumptions and statements.*
Often, participants, including facilitators, enter into a restorative justice process with different ideas about outcomes. We all have different experiences in life. Participants will have different experiences—leading to diverse descriptions—of the conflict event. As a restorative justice practitioner, remember to respect people's perspectives and opinions, even if you do not agree with them. Facilitators ensure a safe, respectful process; participants are the decision-makers, creating outcomes suitable to their needs.

We also strive to challenge our own ageist assumptions. We may think what we are saying is nice, but it could actually be ageist and impact an older adult's self-confidence by serving to make them feel invisible.

The "Old Women's Project" in San Diego, California, developed by Mannie Garza, Janice Keaffaber, and Cynthia Rich, is a wonderful project that confronts ageism. The Old Women's Project reclaims the word "old" as a good thing because, in their words: ". . . we are tired of people sparing us the embarrassment of acknowledging who we really are. It's the manager of the grocery store saying, 'How are you doing, young lady?' It's the woman who gives you a vision test and asks, in a pained voice, as if she were asking about STDs, 'Would you mind *terribly* if I asked you your age?' It's the desk clerk at Motel 6 who says, 'I *hate* to ask, but are you a member of AARP [American Association of Retired Persons]?' These messages, over and over and over, tell you that who you are is awful, an embarrassment to the world and surely one to yourself."[32] The Old Women's Project illustrates how placing emphasis on youth or being embarrassed about somebody's age actually informs how we understand age and reinforces ageist assumptions that old is inferior to young.

Another example provided by the Old Women's Project highlights these assumptions in a different way: "You are a political activist in your early 70s, in excellent health, and you run into a young man in his early 30s whom you haven't seen for a while. You worked together a few years ago on a social justice issue, and you were on a panel with him where your topic was ageism. He comes up to you, and you have a friendly conversation. He tells you about his current political work and you tell him

> about yours. As you are saying goodbye, he takes your arm and says, 'I'm so glad you're still up and around!' He thinks he has said something really nice. But you are left in a kind of shock. You suddenly realize that he sees you in some entirely different way than you supposed. In the foreground for him is what he imagines as your imminent collapse. It's not that you don't want to be reminded of your mortality, it's that you realize that's the glass through which he saw you during your conversation. And if he sees you that way—this bright, progressive young man who's heard your rap about ageism—that must be how many other people see you, not for who you are now but for the terrible abyss they see you about to fall into."[33]

Ageism appears in subtle or subconscious ways in how we speak to older adults. It is important to be mindful about the assumptions we make and conscious about correcting ourselves in how we understand and interact with older adults in our communities.

8. Know your personal boundaries.

Our personal boundaries are the limits we set for our physical, emotional, and social space. At CJI, we have witnessed volunteers who have blurred or crossed professional boundaries; for example, where they began to view the older adult as the mother they wished they had. It can become easy to ignore the need for professional emotional boundaries when a volunteer has not worked through their own grief and loss.

Boundaries Continuum

Too Rigid　　　　　Healthy　　　　　Too Porous

Boundaries Continuum, Example 1: Restorative justice facilitator role boundaries.

Advocate	Mediator	Counselor
Arbitrator	Circle Facilitator	Confidante

Boundaries Continuum, Example 2: Restorative justice facilitator responsibilities.

Director	**Professional**	**Friendship**
• Controlling everything (process and outcomes).	• Friendly while allowing participants to shape process and outcomes.	• Taking on the role of support person or over-identifying with participants' stories.

Boundaries Continuum, Example 3: Participant offers a gift to the facilitator.

Refuse gift without acknowledging appreciation.	Refuse gift, but acknowledge the kindness and generosity of the participant.	Accept gift.

As restorative justice practitioners, it is important that we consistently remind ourselves that our work is not to become the older adult's support person, but to enable the older adult to strengthen their own connections with their own support group. Conversely, we have also experienced volunteers with too-rigid boundaries where they appear cold and impersonal because they are afraid of being too friendly. At CJI, our training describes a continuum of personal boundaries: from too rigid to healthy to too porous. We continually emphasize safe, friendly, and healthy personal boundaries with our staff and volunteers, to ensure that they are applied appropriately to each individual and unique situation.

Persons with Dementia

The Alzheimer's Association in the United States describes dementia as "an illness that affects the brain and eventually causes a person to lose the ability to perform daily self-care. All areas of daily living are affected over the course of the disease. Over time, a person with dementia loses the ability to learn new information, make decisions, and plan the future. Communication with other people becomes difficult. People with dementia ultimately lose the ability to perform daily tasks and to recognize the world around them."[34]

Having dementia should not prohibit someone from participating in restorative justice. However, the Alzheimer's Association has published a series of best practice recommendations for professionals working with individuals who are experiencing dementia. We try to follow these in our restorative justice work.

- Participants with dementia will require an increased emphasis on *preparatory* work, to ensure we investigate how they can and want to participate. We get to know the older adult by talking with them and the people who know them best.
- When we *connect* with people with dementia, our goal is always to leave them feeling calm, reassured, and safe.
- When *communicating*, we are sure to use a gentle tone, a smile, and lots of positive words. We talk with them as adults so that they are recognized as an equal and empowered member in the process. We talk slowly and do no interrupt. We focus more on a person's feelings rather than the details of a story.
- We make sure we offer *choices* but do not overwhelm them with too many options.

In sum, we treat them with the dignity and respect that they deserve.

Conclusion

In this chapter, we discussed aging issues and how we should approach older adults in restorative justice processes. We now have the foundational knowledge that we need to explore real examples of using restorative justice practices with older adults in conflict and abuse situations. In the following four chapters, we will explore how restorative justice works through individual case studies, reflecting on real stories and situations that have occurred in our work in Elder Mediation Services at CJI.

SECTION II
Case Studies of Restorative Justice with Older Adults

5.
Case Study 1
Elder Abuse

In this chapter, we will explore a restorative justice approach to elder abuse. Elder abuse situations can be very challenging as we need to ensure that our process does not create further harm for the participants. To explain how we deal with these challenges, we will tell the story of Ellie and describe how our service responded.

> **Elder abuse** can be defined as "a single, or repeated act, or lack of appropriate action, occurring within any relationship where there is an expectation of trust which causes harm or distress to an older person."[35] Elder abuse can take various forms such as physical, psychological/emotional, sexual, and/or financial abuse. It can also be the result of intentional or unintentional neglect.

Ellie's Story

Ellie was always strongly independent, with a passion for travel and nature. In early adulthood, she often reflected how happy she was about life. Ellie's husband and soulmate, James, was a successful businessman. Together, they raised five children—Fred, Bill, Daniel, Patty, and Ingrid—and exposed them to the joys of nature, as well as the excitement and adventure of world travel.

When James died at the age of 63 from a brain tumour, Ellie, although devastated and heartbroken, managed to resume her independent and energetic lifestyle. However, at age 71, Ellie suffered a stroke. Partially paralyzed, experiencing some vision and memory loss, Ellie was nevertheless reluctant to eschew the independence that had long been her trademark. Before leaving the hospital, she was determined to manage on her own. Weeks later, she recognized that complete independence was not possible and that she needed help with both her personal care and finances. Ellie appointed her two daughters, Patty and Ingrid, as power of attorney for her property and personal care with the stipulation that only certain tasks be fulfilled on her behalf while she was still capable of making her own decisions.

Her eldest daughter, Patty, was single and a successful businesswoman, strongly independent like her mother, and a frequent business traveller. Ingrid, meanwhile, was married with three children and a grandchild, all of whom lived in her household, and worked part-time. Both daughters lived in the same town as Ellie, while her three sons did not.

Faced with her many health issues, Ellie and her daughters decided it made the most sense for her to move in with Ingrid and her family. Things worked well at first.

Family members eagerly supported Ellie, contributing in many different ways to support her through the transition and make her comfortable in her new living space. However, the initial flurry of excitement began to wane, and several months after the move, Patty began to recognize a difference in her mother's demeanor. Once energetic and jovial, Ellie now seemed quiet and depressed and appeared disheveled and unkempt.

When confronted with Patty's inquiries about their mother's situation, Ingrid became angry and directed her sister to mind her own business, assuring her that there was nothing wrong with Ellie. In addition, Ingrid suggested that Patty no longer visit without calling first to schedule a mutually convenient time. Patty was concerned and decided to call her brothers to discuss the situation. Fred refused to get involved, Bill was concerned but did not want to speak with Ingrid, and Daniel expressed anger and called Ingrid to ask about their mother's well-being. After speaking with Daniel, Ingrid was very upset and called Patty, forbidding any further visits with Ellie.

Searching for any way to address the growing conflict, Patty decided to call Community Justice Initiatives' Elder Mediation Service (EMS) program. EMS determined if service was appropriate for the program. In this situation, with the information provided, there was no immediate danger to Ellie to constitute a referral to the Elder Abuse Response Team (EART), a local team made up of a police officer and social worker and linked to a wider network of support services for older adults. While Ellie had the capability of making her own decisions, she had appointed Ingrid and Patty to act on her behalf for certain stipulated tasks as her power of attorney.

As Ingrid was not responding to calls from Patty, EMS connected with Daniel to determine ways to contact Ellie. Daniel informed EMS staff that he was determined to resolve the situation, adding that he had spoken with a lawyer. When told about the potential benefits of a restorative justice process, Daniel agreed to participate. After some persuasion from Daniel, his other brothers also agreed to participate.

Tensions continued to rise within the family, however, when Daniel sought to take Ellie away for a weekend. Ingrid became angry and initially refused the outing, only relenting when Daniel threatened to call the police. Daniel then told his mother about EMS and arranged a hotel room for a meeting to take place with EMS facilitators.

Ellie was then able to tell her story. She spoke about how she initially lived in an upstairs room in Ingrid's home but had since been moved into a basement room with minimal light, no telephone, and only access to a tiny washroom with a toilet and sink. Given her limited mobility, she told the facilitators, she could only manage to climb the stairs once a day in order to enjoy a more comfortable setting and daylight above. She told them that Ingrid, her husband, and two of their children left for work early in the morning while their daughter, Vera, stayed home with their two-year-old grandchild. There was so much early morning commotion upstairs, she lamented, that sleep was difficult at best. She explained how she tried to manage her personal needs on her own, but that was increasingly difficult because she had to climb additional stairs to an upper level bathroom with a shower.

At 11 a.m. every day, she explained, she would go upstairs to get something to eat, only to be chastised by

60

Vera for being clumsy, smelly, or gluttonous. Vera, she told them, made excuses as to why she could not use the phone. Vera was also very impatient with her and sometimes pushed her. To avoid Vera, Ellie spent most of her days alone in the basement, sleeping or watching television.

Ellie told the facilitators that Ingrid would bring her supper downstairs each day, explaining it was easier for her and also quieter. Ingrid would then come down before bedtime to take away the dishes and stay for ten minutes watching TV with her. She said that when she tried to talk to Ingrid about Vera's verbal abuse and the pushing, her daughter accused her of lying. Adding to this already difficult situation, Ellie had also noticed that Ingrid was asking her to sign more checks than usual as part of her contribution to the household budget.

When asked if she was connected with any other community supports, Ellie said that, even though she was not, she would be interested in connecting with a local service organization. EMS helped her connect to the community support agency, one that matched older adults with volunteer visitors. The volunteer later became involved in the restorative justice process as another support for Ellie.

Following the initial meeting, Ingrid and Vera were contacted and invited to participate. Facilitators met with each family member separately ensuring an opportunity to tell their respective stories. They spoke about how their mother's situation impacted them and discussed ways each individual could help resolve the key issues. Facilitators also visited with Ellie, who had since moved into Patty's home, to prepare her to participate in the process.

A peacemaking circle was arranged.[36] *Facilitators welcomed all participants into the circle, opening ceremonies were performed, introductions were made, and roles and guiding principles were reviewed. All participants were given the opportunity to tell their story from their perspective. They discussed what was said, what needed to happen to resolve the issues, and what each was prepared to contribute towards an eventual plan in regards to Ellie's future care.*

The information was recorded in the following Memorandum of Understanding:

> Daniel and Patty will take Ellie to look at retirement residences of her choice, so she can participate in activities, receive support with her personal care needs, and have someone monitor her medication.
>
> Ingrid has apologized for taking additional money from Ellie and agrees to pay it back in installments.
>
> Vera has apologized for the harm she has done to Ellie.
>
> Ellie will meet with a lawyer to change her power of attorney to reflect Patty and Daniel as her power of attorneys.
>
> Ellie will spend scheduled times with Fred, Bill, and Daniel throughout the year.

A Restorative Response

Providing Opportunities to Transform Relationships Through Dialogue and Accountability

In the case of Ellie and her children, the restorative justice process was used to bring the family together to have a deep and honest conversation regarding the health, safety, and well-being of their mother under Ingrid's care. Unlike many formal

Restorative justice seeks to build understanding and restore relationships.

justice processes that focus on placing blame and seeking retribution, the restorative justice process sought to build understanding, alter perspectives, and restore relationships. By focusing on punishment and wrongdoing, the formal justice system often neglects to include the voice of the older adult and rarely takes into consideration their needs or relationships in producing an outcome.

It is important to note that restorative justice processes do not overlook or dismiss the pain or the needs of the responsible party in an elder abuse situation. In fact, the process seeks to give voice to the "wrong-doer" and supports a sense of personal healing and reflection. As was illustrated with Ingrid and Vera, they needed to take responsibility and face the family with a deep and painful confession—a situation that usually tears a family apart. With the implementation of a restorative process, the family was able to communicate and hear one another in a respectful way and seek solutions that would not isolate or abandon anyone. Keeping in mind that many cases of elder abuse are committed by family members or someone close to the older adult and in a position of trust, it is paramount that we promote restoration and healing to strengthen family relation-ships if desired.

Restorative justice for elder abuse cases puts a significant amount of attention on the sensitive and often complex needs of the older adult, while also not dismissing the needs and voice of the responsible party. The process is transformative, healing, and promotes autonomy for the older adult and responsible party to develop a plan to prevent re-victimization and re-offending.

Involving the Community

In Ellie's case, there were two ways the community became involved in the restorative justice process: first, through the volunteer facilitator, and second, through working with community service providers.

At CJI, we involve community members in a meaningful way to create opportunities for healing and resolution in situations of crime, conflict, and abuse. Rather than over-professionalizing our activities, CJI staff equip and support well-trained volunteers to carry out frontline work. In Ellie's case, the process was facilitated by a CJI staff person, together with a volunteer community member. The community member had been trained in the peace-making circle process and as a mediator and had also been instructed to be aware of the impacts of aging on restorative justice services. We carefully screen volunteers and monitor their work. By involving the community, volunteers are better able to understand the needs of older adults and their families and are much more engaged in the process of creating an age-friendly community.

We also work closely with community service providers as part of a continuum of services for older adults. For Ellie's situation, we were able to make sure that a restorative process was a safe choice. However, if there had been immediate concerns for Ellie's safety, we would have referred the situation to the local Elder Abuse Response Team. We also helped to connect Ellie to a visitor program in our community to increase her support network. It is important to create a continuum of responses and choices for the older adult in order to be able to best respond to diverse situations.

Safety, Autonomy, and Dignity

Ellie's story demonstrates the importance of including as many people as possible who care about the older adult. This practice ensures that there are many advocates who are aware of the situation and thus can help provide safety by monitoring the situation to ensure that abusive behavior does not reoccur. Ellie's autonomy and dignity were considered throughout by being given information, as well as choices.

Elder Abuse and Restorative Justice

It is estimated that one in five Canadians know someone who may be experiencing some form of elder abuse. In the United States, reports indicate that one in ten older adults are victims of elder abuse. In such situations, the older adult is commonly isolated, intimidated, dominated, or controlled by the person using abuse and on whom they depend. The abuse can be psychological (intimidation, humiliation, harassment, etc.), physical (shoving, overmedicating/undermedicating, etc.), or financial (withholding money, forging signatures, stealing or misusing

older adult's money).[37] The power and control wheel
graphic that follows helps to illustrate the different
ways abuse is enacted.

Power and Control Wheel:
Abuse in Later Life

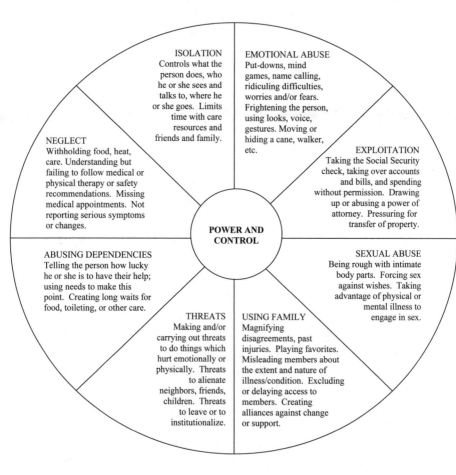

Adopted from the Domestic Abuse Intervention Project, Duluth, MN.

In many cases, the person who has used abuse is a family member or someone who the older adult trusts and has a close relationship with. For example, Statistics Canada (2013) reports that older adult victims of family violence are most likely to be victimized by their own adult children. In fact, about four in ten older adult victims of police-reported family violence indicated that the accused was their grown child; spouses (28%) were the second most likely family members to be identified as perpetrators of family violence against seniors.[38] In the United States, 90% of elder abuse and neglect cases are by a family member, with the highest rate of perpetration by the older adult's children and spouse.[39]

Elder abuse is often not reported. Research suggests that this is due to the older adult's fear of fracturing the relationship with the abuser as well as potential ramifications.[40] Often, older adults will not report due to a belief that they will then have to charge the person who has used abuse.

Considering the significant number of elder abuse cases perpetrated by family members (or someone close to the older adult), utilizing a process that addresses the harm while focusing on the relationship needs of the participants is paramount. Restorative justice processes bring parties together, where safe and appropriate, to discuss the current situation (the harm), the impact it has on the parties (family and friends connected to the older adult), and how the group will move forward, ensuring the best interests of the older adult.

Acknowledging that two of the foundational pieces of a restorative justice philosophy are *restoring* and *healing* participants, it is clear to see how such a process can truly help families and older adults unmask and understand some of the complexities and painful realities often inherent in abuse situations.

Elder abuse situations are very complex. However, with careful consideration of safety issues, restorative processes can provide opportunities for healing and improving circumstances for older adults.

6.
Case Study 2
Decision-Making Later in Life

Restorative justice dialogue processes can be highly effective in helping families plan for issues, even complex ones, related to older adults, such as end-of-life care, power of attorney, and wills. In this chapter, we examine two case studies where restorative justice practices were used to help families make decisions for the future. After telling the stories, we describe the restorative elements in these situations. The restorative process affords families the opportunity to work together to fulfill the choices older adults make in determining their future care.

Shaminder and Laila's Story

Shaminder and Laila have been married for 41 years and enjoyed good physical health, having lived an active life that included swimming, tai chi, bingo, and, as part of their involvement with an adult recreation center, various information sessions. One such information session they attended dealt with the rights of older adults and the importance of having a will and a power of attorney.

Shaminder and Laila decided that they should discuss the topic with their grown children, Diwan and Chandeep, in order to be better prepared for the future. Shaminder and Laila were shocked to find that their children did not, in any way, want to discuss this with them. Diwan said he was too uncomfortable with the topic, and Chandeep refused, saying it was too disturbing to talk about the possibility of her parents dying.

Distressed by their children's reactions, concerned about what their future care would look like, and unsure about how to proceed, Shaminder reached out to extended family for support. Shaminder's brother, Vijay, had heard of CJI's Elder Mediation Service (EMS) and suggested he talk to somebody there for help on their next steps.

EMS facilitators met with everyone involved in the conflict to ensure that a restorative justice process was safe for all participants and to prepare everyone for a meeting. Before everyone met together in a larger group, it was agreed that Diwan and Chandeep would attend the same adult recreation center information session that had motivated Shaminder and Laila to talk to them in the first place. By doing so, each member of the family would come prepared for the meeting with the same information about wills and power of attorney.

After the information session, EMS facilitators met again with everyone as a last check-in to ensure that all family members were still in agreement to meet each other. Despite Diwan and Chandeep still struggling with their emotions around the subject, the family agreed to meet. The facilitators helped the family through a dialogue process of sharing their fears and hopes for the future. Tears *were shed, but concrete plans were set for the next steps, and the family felt connected to each other again.*

Abasi's Story

Malika's father, Abasi, was diagnosed with early dementia more than a year ago.

Despite his insistence that he live on his own and tend to his own needs, it had become apparent that Abasi could no longer do so. In fact, at one point he became hospitalized because he had neglected to take his medication—insulin for diabetes. A doctor's assessment confirmed what family members already suspected: Abasi was no longer capable of managing his own care needs nor making important decisions for himself. The doctor advised that Abasi move into a long-term care facility in order to receive the assistance he needed.

Malika and her older brother, Kendi, had been appointed power of attorney for Abasi's personal care and property. They had two younger sisters, Bisa and Shani, who seldom got along with Kendi. Distressed by the conflict that surrounded these difficult decisions, Malika contacted EMS in the hopes of bringing her family together to talk about their father's needs and how to proceed with his personal care, place of residence, and various financial and property issues.

After meeting individually with the siblings to hear each of their stories and perspectives and to consider a range of potential solutions, EMS facilitators connected with Abasi. Although not capable of participating in the discussion regarding his future care needs, he was still consulted throughout the process.

EMS invited all the siblings into a peacemaking circle. After the initial introductions and discussions about circle

71

guidelines, the siblings each shared their stories without interruption. The facilitators then asked participants to respond to what they had heard from their family members. Their emotions were high, including anger. Some discussion revolved around the past, where siblings felt they had experienced the favoritism and dominance of some members over others. While allowing for the expression of complicated feelings about their pasts, facilitators helped guide conversation toward decisions about their father's care, keeping the focus on the best interests of their father. In order for participants to not feel disregarded for sharing deep-seated feelings associated with the past, facilitators offered the siblings the opportunity to address those issues at a later date. When Malika shared the doctor's diagnosis and recommendations related to Abasi's early dementia, her younger siblings voiced their cynicism and distrust. Malika suggested they call the doctor, and the siblings agreed. Abasi's doctor was able to explain the diagnosis, provide thorough information, and answer the siblings' questions. Now fully understanding the situation and what it meant for Abasi, the conversation between the siblings turned to the decisions that were necessary in order to address their father's formidable needs.

In the end, the decisions were recorded in a Memorandum of Understanding, which served as a tangible reminder to all the participants about their ability to work together to make decisions in the best interests of their father.

Facilitators also invited the siblings to a circle meeting that included their father. Abasi was included as an equal participant in the second circle, in order to give him a sense of involvement while witnessing the unity of his family. In a much more relaxed atmosphere, devoid of anger and blame, the siblings, one by one, were given an opportunity to talk to and offer words of encouragement and love for their father.

A Restorative Response

Providing Opportunities to Address the Needs of the Participants

In the case studies above, we have emphasized the importance that restorative justice places upon creating a safe space for identifying and addressing participants' needs. When families are faced with the difficult task of helping their loved ones prepare for the future, it can be an emotional, confusing, and difficult time for all those involved. Family dynamics, histories, and other various relational factors within families will influence restorative justice outcomes.

Taking on the role of making difficult decisions regarding the future of an older parent is an often daunting prospect, filled with complicated emotions, including grief. Indeed, decision-making can be a source of major family conflict and shattered relationships. Each of the stories above describes some of the challenges families experience when making decisions on behalf of an older adult. The story of Shaminder and Laila highlights the needs, challenges, and experiences from the older adult's perspective, while the story of Malika and her family demonstrates the needs and experiences from the perspective of an adult child making a decision for an older parent who is no longer able to do so.

In the case of Diwan and Chandeep, who were approached to assist their parents in their end-of-life care plan, it is clear that much of their uneasiness and discomfort came from a place of vulnerability and fear. The restorative process was an effective avenue to open communication in times of high emotion and discomfort in order to build understanding among the family members. The process also allowed time for the family

> **An opportunity for openness helps break down barriers to communication.**

to communicate with each other about how difficult these issues were for all of them and allowed participants to identify what support was needed. This opportunity led to empowerment, the validation of emotions and perspectives, and opportunity for stronger relationships.

Hopefully, in a restorative space, participants can truly talk about what they are feeling and trust that they will be heard and treated with respect. Through storytelling and perspective sharing, families are able to give voice to what they are experiencing. The stories and emotions they share may relate to the issue at hand (making big decisions for their older parent) or they may relate to events and family experiences in the past. An opportunity for openness helps break down barriers to communication, so participants can move forward, while at the same time developing a plan for aging parents reflective of their values, needs, and wishes.

Providing Opportunities for Accountability
Another key principle of restorative justice is accountability. In restorative processes, the participants are

accountable to each other. As illustrated in the stories above, the family members were asked to offer their ideas and solutions to contribute toward outcomes. In the presence of siblings, they agreed to take on certain tasks and responsibilities, so that they all were accountable to live up to their commitments.

Providing Opportunities to Experience Dignity

Despite capacity limitations faced by some older adults, as in the case of Abasi, and although certain individuals may not be able to participate in the same way as others, everyone has an opportunity to experience dignity through resolution. Older adults with limitations are encouraged to express their feelings in any way possible. As such, when loved ones gather to discuss their situation and explore their needs, the best interests of the older adult remain at the forefront. The practice provides those with limitations a sense of belonging, respect, value, and dignity.

Involving Older Adult Community Agencies and Professionals in the Process

For most restorative justice practices, involving community members is a core value. For example, in Abasi's story, the doctor was consulted by the family during the circle process. In the restorative justice process, we encourage professionals to participate in the peacemaking circle in some way (e.g. through telephone or in person), as it is important for the family to hear the same information at the same time and for the professionals to gain more information about the family capacity to care for the older adult.

In this chapter, our stories exemplified that decision-making in later life can be difficult for families and older adults. Restorative justice processes can provide opportunities for families to share information and make decisions in inclusive, safe ways that respect everyone's dignity.

7.
Case Study 3
Caregiver Burnout

There are many people in North America and beyond providing informal, or unpaid, care for an older adult. In fact, the National Alliance for Caregiving and AARP estimate about 34.2 million people in the United States are informal caregivers of older adults.[41] Caregiving can be a demanding and stressful task, and can lead to high levels of stress, depression, exhaustion and health issues for the caregiver. Steven Zarit, in his research on family caregivers, stated that "40% to 70% of family caregivers have clinically significant symptoms of depression with approximately a quarter to half of these caregivers meeting the diagnostic criteria for major depression."[42] Restorative justice processes can provide a place for people to safely talk about their needs as a caregiver. In this chapter, we tell the story of Anna, Rebecca, and their family, explaining how our service helped them dialogue about caregiver burnout.

Anna's Story

Anna, a happily married, 32-year-old mother of two, had always enjoyed a close and loving relationship with her single mother, Rebecca. Now that her 62-year-old mother had been diagnosed with early dementia, it seemed perfectly natural for her to move into Anna's home.

Anna's life was busy, if not hectic. Her sales executive husband, Kevin, travelled frequently for his job. Her children, eight and twelve years old, were active in a host of school and extracurricular activities. Faced with her additional responsibility and eager to accommodate her mother and her new caregiving role that required her to spend more time at home, she quit her full-time job and took on a part-time position.

Despite the adjustment to new challenges and new routines, everything went reasonably well, at least for a while. Then Rebecca had a nasty fall, which significantly reduced her mobility and independence. Due to her new physical limitations, Rebecca increasingly relied on Anna. This also coincided with increased dementia-related symptoms, growing forgetfulness, and confusion. Family members noticed that Rebecca seemed depressed, frustrated, and frequently moody. As Anna was forced to devote more time to her mother's care, other family responsibilities were being overlooked, and the relationship with her husband and children became strained. Anna was slowly becoming burnt out.

Kelly, Rebecca's sister and a frequent visitor to the household, couldn't help but notice the family tension and stress caused by Rebecca's difficult needs and the high level of care being required from Anna. Kelly discussed with Rebecca the possibility of her moving into a retirement home where Rebecca's needs could more easily be met. Rebecca agreed. However, Anna heavily objected to the decision and became furious at Kelly, accusing her of interference. Through this difficult situation, Anna's relationship with her mother was significantly harmed.

Aware that she had named Anna and Kelly powers of attorney for her personal care and her property, Rebecca now worried that her daughter and her sister would not be able to work together in her best interests when she became incapable of making her own decisions. After discussing her situation with a community support agency caseworker, Rebecca decided to call CJI's Elder Mediation Service (EMS) program.

By participating in a restorative justice process, Rebecca was able to openly and safely talk about her concerns with her daughter and her sister. She told Anna that she hated being a burden on her family and expressed feelings of sadness and loneliness at the loss of what had been a loving and close relationship with her daughter. During this process, Anna was able to express her concern about future decisions that needed to be made on her mother's behalf that would be in her best interests and also not cause conflict and more harm.

Anna expressed her grief at the harmed relationship with her mother. She spoke about feelings of guilt and failure because she was unable to manage Rebecca's care on her own. She apologized to Kelly for her anger and acknowledged that she assumed Kelly's actions were because she was jealous of Anna's relationship with Rebecca.

Kelly, meanwhile, was able to express that her motivation to encourage Rebecca to move into a nursing home came from a genuine concern for the strain on Anna and her family.

With increased understanding of each participant's concerns, healing had begun. In addition, issues regarding Rebecca's ongoing care were resolved. Facilitators helped participants write a Memorandum of Understanding to remind participants of the discussions and the decisions they had made.

A Restorative Response

Being a sole caregiver for an older parent with declining health can be emotionally and physically overwhelming. In the story above, despite good intentions, Anna's attempts to manage family responsibilities at the same time as the formidable care needs of her aging mother caused her to burn out, unable to adequately meet her relational obligations to either. Others took notice that some outside intervention might be necessary to preserve the well-being of all parties and to ensure the necessary care is provided for the older adult. Restorative justice as a response to caregiver burnout can be an effective way to open dialogue and allow people to make some decisions. It offers caregivers like Anna a safe space to talk openly about their needs, concerns, and challenges as they strive to assume responsibilities in a healthy way.

In a restorative justice process, Community Justice Initiatives (CJI) seeks to support the older adult and those in caregiver roles in such a way that they may express how their particular situation impacts their lives and that they may identify some of the feelings they are experiencing. CJI asks participants questions such as:

- [To the caregiver] What is your role as a caregiver to the older adult?

- [To the older adult] Describe your relationship with your caregiver.
- What is your daily routine?
- What about your role or daily routine has been difficult, and what has been working well?
- What stress are you experiencing, and how has it impacted your life and your other relationships?
- Where has the most stress been, and what do you need to reduce this stress?
- Who else has a relationship with you (family, faith community, friends, neighbors, caseworkers, etc.)? Can we talk with them?
- What would you like to communicate to each other?
- What would an improved future relationship look like?
- What might you like to say to each other about improving your relationship?

Acknowledging the experiences of others can lead participants to feel a sense of empowerment and validation of their own feelings in a difficult time, and create a space for increased understandings and empathy. Ultimately, by addressing caregiver burn-out through dialogue, participants have an opportunity to hear the experiences of others and gain insight into how a caregiver is coping. Everyone can better figure out how to work together in a way that is more sustainable.

Often, in restorative processes, the process is as meaningful as the outcome. When faced with difficult situations and responsibilities, people feel disconnected or isolated from other important people in their lives. EMS allows the caregiver to have a voice and be heard. Caregivers can trust facilitators to guide a respectful, safe meeting.

Upholding and ensuring the best interests of the older adult is paramount in any of CJI's processes. When a caregiver feels overwhelmed and unable to provide optimal care, older adults are increasingly vulnerable to potentially dangerous situations. In a restorative approach, partic-ipants must share respon-

The process is as meaningful as the outcome.

sibility and form solutions together to ensure the well-being of the caregiver, alongside the older adult.

In this chapter, we discussed a restorative justice response to caregiver burnout. We know that, in life, many people become caregivers to older adults. It is normal for caregivers to experience the challenges that Anna faced in that role. As we have discussed in this chapter, restorative justice processes provide a space where all needs are heard, considered, and addressed.

8.
Case Study 4
A Community in Conflict

In this chapter, we will describe our work with communities in conflict—when conflict moves beyond the interpersonal to involving many people. More specifically, you will read about Community Justice Initiatives' (CJI) work in older adult housing community residences, including retirement homes and rent-subsidy housing, that are experiencing conflict. Our experience shows that when residents feel unsafe in their homes, it is stressful for older adults and contributes to a "toxic" living environment.

As explained in Chapter 3, CJI began working with older adults at the request of their landlords by mediating conflicts between neighbors. Significantly, we would frequently be called back to the same buildings but to help different neighbors. Through this experience, we realized that in order to effect lasting change, we would have to get at root causes of conflict. The interpersonal conflicts were actually symptoms of a culture where residents were feeling isolated. We needed to help create a new culture, one with stronger relational connections where everyone felt like they belonged and mattered. However, this meant that, as restorative justice practitioners, we needed more tools than mediation, which is better suited for resolving interpersonal conflicts. As a result, we began creating and providing restorative justice programming for everyone who lived in a building (approximately 30 to 100 people).

The following are steps to take when working with a community of older adults:

1. When we receive a conflict resolution request from a housing provider, facilitators meet with organizational employees to **understand the issues** and determine what, if any, interventions may have already been attempted.

2. Facilitators visit the residence alongside a representative of the housing provider and **go door-to-door** to introduce Elder Mediation Service (EMS) to tenants. EMS then contacts the tenants and schedules individual meetings.

3. **Initial visits** with tenants are an opportunity to get to know them while gaining understanding of the issues from their perspective. It is important to allow the individual time to share their concerns, express their needs, and suggest possible solutions to the relevant issues.

4. EMS facilitators can then assess and **explore resolutions and strategies**. Strategies can include mediation, individual conflict coaching, talking and/or healing circles, community circles,

restorative justice circles, relationship-building events, skill building, and support groups, as well as information-sharing events. Other agencies, which can provide additional support to the tenants, may also be introduced.

5. Finally, EMS develops partnerships with other housing providers, police, and various community support agencies to **establish a "Community Living Partnership Committee."** The committee meets quarterly to seek ways to support, exchange knowledge, and empower the community to feel safe, included, valued, and accepted, regardless of differences.

Theodore's Story

Theodore's life took a drastic turn in the aftermath of his wife's death. He became overwhelmed with grief and found it difficult to cope with changes to his daily life. Tenants in the older adult residence he had lived in for the past eight years offered to help. Theodore refused help. He wanted to remain independent.

Several months after his wife's death, housing officials began to receive complaints from other tenants. Someone, they complained, had repeatedly knocked on their doors in the wee hours of the morning. Others said their newspapers were disappearing, while others cited feces in the washing machines and spilled coffee on the foyer carpet. Officials tried to meet with the tenants, but their anger and mounting frustration precluded any meaningful dialogue. The residents wanted action, not talk. In an effort to determine the source of the objectionable behavior, officials installed cameras to monitor the building. The culprit was Theodore. When confronted by officials, however, Theodore became angrier, and his erratic behavior increased. Theodore's neighbors, now aware of Theodore's actions, targeted him with gossip and verbal disdain, to which Theodore responded with curses and threats.

Desperate to address the situation, officials contacted EMS. In Theodore's residential building, EMS had already been involved with helping residents run weekly social, games, and activities time.

After meeting with officials to learn about the issues and determine what interventions had already been attempted, EMS staff connected with Theodore. It was immediately evident that he was having difficulty living on his own. His apartment was filthy, he appeared unkempt, and he spoke in a halting and incoherent manner.

EMS staff decided to arrange a meeting that would include representatives from local and relevant community service agencies (e.g., those relating to mental health and older adult care) to determine ways to support Theodore. They developed a support team and agreed that Theodore's situation required immediate attention.

EMS staff also met with tenants in a community peacemaking circle process to give them an opportunity to address the impact of Theodore's behavior. When told of the support team that had been established and the steps to be taken to address the situation, tenants were heartened, agreeing to proceed and providing a list of requests for the support team to consider.

EMS met regularly with the tenants, offering ongoing support, listening to their stories, addressing their issues, and offering various activities to enhance their conflict resolution skills and rebuild a sense of community. At the same time, the support team met with Theodore, providing him with much-needed assistance.

Several weeks later, in an attempt to re-integrate Theodore into the resident community, EMS established a healing circle so he could meet with some of his neighbors. He apologized for his behavior and the tenants reciprocated, acknowledging that they did not understand his situation.

Subsequently, after the healing circle, whenever neighbors offered help, Theodore gladly accepted.

A Restorative Response

Providing Opportunities to Express Needs in a Safe Way

Conflict can occur when the actions that an individual takes to express themselves and get their needs met interfere or impose upon another's needs. When we think of a community where a variety of different perceptions, needs, and ideas come together, it is easy to see how conflict can emerge. A restorative process helps people find ways to express their needs and have them met.

In Theodore's story, there were several processes used to address the different needs. First, the community's residents needed a productive way to talk about their fears instead of gossiping or fear-mongering. To talk about what had happened, they used a community peacemaking circle (see Chapter 2 for further description). Secondly, Theodore needed a safe way to admit that he needed help; Theodore experienced a circle meeting with community providers. Finally, a healing circle was formed to bring together everyone to discuss needs and obligations.

Providing Opportunities for Safe and Productive Dialogue

In situations of community conflict, the longer people are in conflict, the more likely there is a negative "shift" in how community members view each other that in turn affects the "wellness" of a community. As illustrated in the case of Theodore, because of his disruptive behavior and the corresponding gossiping, a shift in perception occurred where Theodore went from being a "neighbor" to "trouble-maker." Amid this shift, community members began voicing their concerns, finding allies, and sharing their perspectives and needs with each other. Neighbors banded together, either for Theodore or against him. Differences between people were exacerbated. A toxic environment resulted, and people felt stress and fear.

What makes communities of older adults particularly prone to conflict is that their members are often not offered the opportunity to come together and voice their perspectives as a whole. Instead, conflict escalates as people tend to fill in knowledge gaps through gossip and blame.

In the case of an older adult population, where many people tend to live in close-knit residential communities, the potential for conflict is high. Shifts occur on a regular basis. In restorative justice practices, the community is allowed to discuss the impact of these shifts. Individuals are encouraged to speak about issues, interests, and needs and to tell their stories. Consequently, the restorative process ensures all voices are heard. The risk of gossip, misinformation, blame, and oppositional group formation is significantly reduced.

Conversations About Accountability and Trust-Building

Conflict often creates and/or encourages a pervasive sense of distrust or uneasiness among community members. One of the most important aspects of a restorative circle is the revelation of the shared interests and needs expressed by community members. Common interests and needs include:

- feeling safe in their homes;
- having a welcoming environment for visitors;
- having neighbors who help each other;
- speaking to each other with kindness and respect;
- understanding of each other's differences.

In restorative justice, participants tell their stories. Relationships are built and strengthened through the identification of shared needs.

In addition, peacemaking circles address issues of accountability, understanding, and trust within the community. A peacemaking circle can help people understand what has actually happened, who is responsible, what their perspectives are, and what will be done to ensure that such disruptive incidents do not reoccur. Through this dialogue, community members have the opportunity to explain how they have been impacted and demonstrate that they are trustworthy members of the community.

When harm occurs in an older adult community, as illustrated in Theodore's case, one of the intentions of a healing circle is to help the older adults move towards a resolution. A restorative circle can serve as a platform for a community to create a resolution that reflects the needs, desires, and hopes of the group while also restoring trust, relationships, and a sense of belonging among all its members. The sense of connection that often results from these processes helps individuals respect each member of the community and care for their well-being.

Involving the Community

In Theodore's story, EMS facilitators involved a larger number of people in the restorative process. Concerned community members were invited to the support group, even if they had not been directly affected by Theodore. Community agencies were also invited to connect with Theodore and were part of the restorative process. The outcome was a small step toward a larger vision. In fact, the tenants began a process of making their building a *restorative community*, where people would be accountable to each other.

In this chapter, we discussed that, when people live in close proximity, conflict affects everyone. Restorative justice processes can strengthen a community's capacity to address the needs and obligations that arise from conflict. As a result, participants can create a stronger community where everyone feels a sense of belonging.

90

9.
Conclusion

The *United Nations World Report on Ageing and Health* challenged all nations to build a new framework of global action for healthy aging. The challenge is to "transcend outdated ways of thinking about ageing, foster a major shift in how we understand ageing and health, and inspire the development of transformative approaches."[43] We believe that a restorative justice approach to older adult abuse and conflict is transformative.

Restorative justice processes include a number of key components to transforming how we help older adults and their families, neighbors, and caregivers talk about aging concerns and work through difficult conflict situations—even elder abuse. As we have discussed throughout this book and illustrated in our case studies, the restorative justice process can help participants face difficult situations. The processes we have described impact the relationships of participants, changing what each individual's role and responsibilities are to each other and themselves, while also transforming their perspectives of the situation. Restorative justice helps to prevent the isolation that many people in conflict feel—especially older adults—by increasing the community's involvement with the older adult and family.

Restorative justice processes do not seek to punish. Retributive styles of punishment tend to reduce feelings of belonging and distract from accountability and transformation. Instead, restorative justice provides opportunities for people to come together to identify and address harms that have occurred and take meaningful actions towards repairing harm done. Restorative justice does not leave people to try to address their needs in isolation. Instead, people are connected with community services, while peacemaking circles bring people together to talk about how they are impacted and how their needs may be addressed. In all of the case studies, involving the community was purposeful and meaningful, not just a by-product of the process, and was achieved through volunteer community members facilitating the restorative justice process or by intentionally connecting people to community services. In fact, we believe the success of Community Justice Initiatives' Elder Mediation Service is rooted in holistic approaches to dealing with older adult conflict and abuse—intentionally connecting as many people as possible, including professionals, family, and friends, with the older adult.

The goals and signposts of restorative justice fit into a wider vision of a transformed community that creates the conditions where restorative justice can work: a future vision where we are all "age friendly" and we seek a restorative response as a *first* response.

Looking to the Future

We continue to discover ways that we can foster a community that is better equipped to help older adults thrive as they age. One of these ways is to support initiatives that are creating age-friendly cities and communities (discussed in Chapter 3). The cities of Waterloo, Kitchener, and Cambridge in Ontario, Canada, where we live and work, are all in different phases of become age-friendly cities. Concretely, this means that the these cities have begun addressing areas that are not "age friendly," including increasing the amount of seating in public spaces, providing longer pedestrian crossing times at certain intersections, ensuring that city services are on public transportation routes, etc.[44, 45, 46] We may not think these policies are important to conflict or abuse, but the absence of policies that consider the needs of older adults creates a culture that does not address the needs of older adults as equal community members and contributes to conditions that allow abuse and conflict to grow. An age-friendly community is also a restorative community.

At Community Justice Initiatives (CJI), one of our goals is to create a "restorative community." There are other communities that have challenged themselves to do similar. Most notably, the city of Hull, in the United Kingdom, first piloted the idea of a "restorative city."[47] Having a "restorative city" means that restorative justice practices and processes are infused into broad city systems that impact the entire community, such as schools, child welfare systems, criminal justice systems, and businesses. CJI's goal is to inspire our community to use a restorative response as a first response to conflict, crime, and abuse. To do this, we also need to influence the systems in which we live to become restorative rather than punitive. This includes working with municipal governments, police departments, schools, retirement homes, and businesses to have a discussion about restorative justice, provide training and learning opportunities about restorative justice to the public, and to assist people to utilize restorative justice in their everyday lives. More importantly, it also means adopting a restorative worldview. If we can influence people to transform their understanding so that the "natural" way to respond to conflict and harm is restorative rather than punitive, it leads us down a different path with radically different actions and outcomes—transformative ones!

In sum, we at CJI and Elder Mediation Service are advocating using restorative justice processes in individual cases of older adult conflict and abuse. However, we also believe that services like ours work best when the community is prepared to act from an age-friendly, restorative perspective. Through this book, we hope we have inspired you to believe that restorative justice can be one tool for us to reimagine how we respond to the opportunities that are occurring as our populations are aging.

We want to end this book with our inspiration, the people we work with—Theodore, Anna, Ellie, and the many others who have courageously confronted the conflict and abuse in their lives—we have learned so much from you. We also thank our colleagues—the volunteers and students—who spend their free time providing quality services to our community.

Further Reading

Alzheimer's Association. *Dementia Care Practice Recommendations for Professionals Working in a Home Setting* (Chicago, IL: Alzheimer's Association, 2009). Available at https://www.alz.org/national/documents/phase_4_home_care_recs.pdf

Groh, Arlene. *A Healing Approach to Elder Abuse and Mistreatment: The Restorative Justice Approaches to Elder Abuse Project* (Kitchener, ON: Community Care Access Centre of Waterloo, 2003).

Hadley, Michael L. (Ed.). *The Spiritual Roots of Restorative Justice* (Albany, NY: State University of New York Press, 2001).

The Old Women's Project. Available at www.oldwomens project.org

Oudshoorn, Judah, Michelle Jackett, and Lorraine Stutzman Amstutz. *The Little Book of Restorative Justice for Sexual Abuse: Hope through Trauma* (New York: Good Books, 2015).

Pranis, Kay. *The Little Book of Circle Processes: A New/Old Approach to Peacemaking.* (Intercourse, PA: Good Books, 2005).

Senior Daybreak of Hilltop. *Dementia Training Manual: A Caregiving Tool for Families and Professionals* (Grand Junction, CO: Senior Daybreak of Hilltop,

2015). Available at http://seniordaybreak.org/wp
-content/uploads/sites/103/2016/12/Dementia-
Training-Manual.pdf

Strang, Heather and John Braithwaite (Eds.). *Restorative Justice and Civil Society* (Cambridge, United Kingdom: Cambridge University Press, 2001).

World Health Organization. *World Report on Ageing and Health* (Geneva, Switzerland: World Health Organization, 2015). Available at http://www.who.int/ageing/publications/world-report-2015/en/

Zehr, Howard. *Changing Lenses* (Kitchener, ON: Herald Press, 1990).

Zehr, Howard. *The Little Book of Restorative Justice: Revised and Updated* (New York: Good Books, 2014).

Endnotes

1 Groh, Arlene. *A Healing Approach to Elder Abuse and Mistreatment: The Restorative Justice Approaches to Elder Abuse Project* (Kitchener, ON: Community Care Access Centre of Waterloo, 2003).

2 Ibid., page 4

3 Hadley, Michael L. (Ed.). *The Spiritual Roots of Restorative Justice* (Albany, NY: State University of New York Press, 2001).

4 Zehr, Howard. *The Little Book of Restorative Justice: Revised and Updated* (New York: Good Books, 2014).

5 Ibid, page 53

6 Ibid, page 19

7 Pranis, Kay. *The Little Book of Circle Processes: A New/Old Approach to Peacemaking* (Intercourse, PA: Good Books, 2005).

8 Braithwaite, John. "Setting Standards for Restorative Justice." *British Journal of Criminology* 42, no. 3 (2002): 563–577.

9 Oudshoorn, Judah, Michelle Jackett, and Lorraine Stutzman Amstutz. *The Little Book of Restorative Justice for Sexual Abuse* (New York: Good Books, 2015).

10 Mayer, Bernard. *The Dynamics of Conflict: A Guide to Engagement and Intervention, 2nd ed.* (San Francisco: Jossey-Bass, 2012), 68.

11 Ibid.
12 Shelly Schanzenbacker, interview, March 1, 2016.
13 Statistics Canada. "National Seniors Day . . . by the numbers," last modified November 09, 2016. Available at http://www.statcan.gc.ca/eng/dai/smr08/2014/smr08_191_2014
14 World Health Organization. *Global Age-Friendly Cities: A Guide* (Geneva, Switzerland: World Health Organization, 2007).
15 Ibid.
16 Arlene Groh, interview, February 18, 2016.
17 World Health Organization. *World Report on Ageing and Health* (Geneva, Switzerland: World Health Organization, 2015), 11. Available at http://www.who.int/ageing/publications/world-report-2015/en/
18 United Nations. "United Nations Principles for Older Persons" (December 1991). Available at http://www.ohchr.org/EN/ProfessionalInterest/Pages/OlderPersons.aspx
19 Quoted by Ken Dychtwald in "Liberating Aging: An Interview with Maggie Kuhn." *New Age* (February 1979).
20 WHO. *World Report on Ageing and Health* (2015), 25.
21 WHO. *World Report on Ageing and Health* (2015), 26.
22 Hepple, R. T. "Impact of Aging on Mitochondrial Function in Cardiac and Skeletal Muscle." *Free Radical Biology and Medicine 98*, September (2016): 177–186.
23 National Institute on Aging. "Biology of Aging Research Today for a Healthier Tomorrow." (Bethesda, MD: National Institute on Aging, 2011). Available

at https://www.nia.nih.gov/health/publication/aging
-under-microscope/what-aging (accessed November
28, 2016)

24 Silk, Susan and American Psychology Association.
"Aging and Depression." Available at http://www
.apa.org/helpcenter/aging-depression.aspx
(accessed November 28, 2016)

25 National Institute on Aging. "Biology of Aging:
Research Today for a Healthier Tomorrow."

26 Silk, Susan and American Psychology Association.
"Aging and Depression."

27 Hayes, Catherine. "How Sociological Perspectives
on Ageing Can Aid Reflection by HCAs." *British
Journal of Healthcare Assistants 8*, no. 5 (2014):
238–244.

28 National Institute on Aging. "Biology of Aging
Research Today for a Healthier Tomorrow."

29 Silk, Susan and American Psychology Association.
"Aging and Depression."

30 Schaie, K. Warner, and Neil Charness. *Impact
of Technology on Successful Aging* (New York:
Springer Publishing Company, 2003).

31 WHO. *World Report on Ageing and Health* (2015),
52.

32 The Old Women's Project. "Real Life Examples of
Ageist Comments: What They Do to Us, How We
Can Respond to Them." Available at http://www.
oldwomensproject.org/real_life.htm (accessed
April 28, 2017).

33 Ibid.

34 Alzheimer's Association. "Dementia Care Practice
Recommendations for Professionals Working
in a Home Setting." (Chicago, IL: Alzheimer's

Association, 2009). Available at: https://www.alz.org/national/documents/phase_4_home_care_recs.pdf

35 World Health Organization. "Elder Abuse." Available at: http://www.who.int/ageing/projects/elder_abuse/en/ (accessed April 28, 2017).

36 Pranis, K. *The Little Book of Circle Processes: A New /Old Approach to Peacemaking.*

37 National Council on Aging. "Elder Abuse Facts." Available at: https://www.ncoa.org/public-policy-action/elder-justice/elder-abuse-facts/ (accessed April 28, 2017).

38 Canadian Centre for Justice Statistics. *Family Violence in Canada: A Statistical Profile, 2013* (Ottawa, ON: Statistics Canada, 2015), 5. Available at: http://www.statcan.gc.ca/pub/85-002-x/2014001/article/14114-eng.pdf

39 National Council on Aging. "Elder Abuse Facts."

40 Canadian Centre for Justice Statistics. *Family Violence in Canada: A Statistical Profile.*

41 AARP and National Alliance for Caregiving. *Caregiving in the U.S.: 2015 Report* (AARP, June 2015).

42 Zarit, Steven H. "Assessment of Family Caregivers: A Research Perspective." In *Caregiver Assessment: Voices and Views from the Field.* Report from a National Consensus Development Conference, Vol. II (2006): 12–37. San Francisco: Family Caregiver Alliance, 2006.

43 WHO. *World Report on Ageing and Health* (2015).

44 City of Waterloo. "Age-Friendly City." (Waterloo, ON: City of Waterloo, 2015). Available at: http://www.waterloo.ca/en/living/agefriendlycity.asp (accessed April 28, 2017).

45 Cambridge Council on Aging. "Age Friendly." (Cambridge, ON: Cambridge Council on Aging, 2013). Available at http://www.cambridgecoa.org/age-friendly/ (accessed May 12, 2017).

46 City of Kitchener. "Age-Friendly Community." (Kitchener, ON: City of Kitchener, 2017). Available at http://www.kitchener.ca/en/livinginkitchener/Age-Friendly-Community.asp (accessed May 12, 2017).

47 Wachtel, Joshua. "World's First 'Restorative City': Hull, UK, Improves Outcomes of All Interventions with Young People, Saves Resources." *International Institute for Restorative Practices*, January, 19, 2012. Available at http://restorativeworks.net/2012/01/restorative-city-hull-uk-takes-restorative-practices-to-the-private-sector/

About the Authors

Julie Friesen is a director of programs at Community Justice Initiatives. She has been involved in conflict resolution, mediation, and management positions since 1997. Julie has conflict resolution experience ranging from elder mediations, workplace conflicts, neighborhood disputes, and criminal court mediations. She holds an MA in sociology from the University of Kansas. She lives in Waterloo, Ontario.

Wendy Meek currently supervises the Elder Mediation Program at Community Justice Initiatives, a nonprofit, restorative justice organization in Kitchener, Canada. Wendy has many years of experience assisting victims and offenders, as well as community members, in addressing and resolving conflict and crime. She facilitates circles, mediations, and groups and is also a passionate speaker on the topic of restorative justice and older adults. She lives in Cambridge, Ontario.

Group Discounts for

The Little Book of Restorative Justice for Older Adults
ORDER FORM

If you would like to order multiple copies of **The Little Book of Restorative Justice for Older Adults** for groups you know or are a part of, please email **bookorders@skyhorsepublishing.com** or fax order to **(212) 643-6819**. (Discounts apply only for more than one copy.)

Photocopy this page and the next as often as you like.

The following discounts apply:

1 copy	$5.99
2-5 copies	$5.39 each (a 10% discount)
6-10 copies	$5.09 each (a 15% discount)
11-20 copies	$4.79 each (a 20% discount)
21-99 copies	$4.19 each (a 30% discount)
100 or more	$3.59 each (a 40% discount)

Free Shipping for orders of 100 or more!

Prices subject to change.

Quantity   **Price**   **Total**

The Little Book of Restorative
_____ copies of **Justice for Older Adults** @   _____   _____
(Standard ground shipping costs will be added for orders of less than 100 copies.)

METHOD OF PAYMENT

❐   Check or Money Order
           *(payable to **Skyhorse Publishing** in U.S. funds)*

❐   Please charge my:
❐ MasterCard ❐ Visa
❐ Discover   ❐ American Express
\# _____

Exp. date and sec. code_____

Signature _____

Name _____

Address _____

City_____

State _____

Zip_____

Phone_____

Email _____

SHIP TO: (if different)
Name _____

Address _____

City_____

State _____

Zip_____

Call: (212) 643-6816
Fax: (212) 643-6819
Email: bookorders@skyhorsepublishing.com
(do not email credit card info)